WINSLOW
HOMER

WINSLOW HOMER

Kate F. Jennings

Crescent Books
A Division of Crown Publishers, Inc.

The 1990 edition published by
Crescent Books, distributed by
Crown Publishers, Inc.
225 Park Avenue South
New York, New York 10003

Produced by
Brompton Books Corp.
15 Sherwood Place
Greenwich, CT 06830
USA

Printed in Hong Kong

ISBN 0-517-01516-1

h g f e d c b a

Page 1:
Waiting for the Start
1889, watercolor, 14×20 in.
Gift of Jesse Metcalf,
Museum of Art, Rhode Island School of
Design, Providence, RI

Page 2:
Kissing the Moon
1904, oil on canvas, 30×40 in.
Bequest of Candace C. Stimson,
Addison Gallery of American Art,
Phillips Academy, Andover, MA

Pages 4-5:
Inside the Bay, Cullercoats
c. 1883, watercolor on paper, 15⅜×28½ in.
Gift of Louise Ryals Arkell,
The Metropolitan Museum of Art, New York,
NY
(54.183)

Contents

INTRODUCTION

Winslow Homer's quiet beginnings may have been the safe harbor that in later years would sustain him in the mastery of his chosen craft. He was primarily a self-taught painter, with few flamboyant gestures in either his artistic style or personal life. His visions of the Civil War, his watercolors of nineteenth-century genre figures, Adirondack retreats and tropical landscapes, and especially the powerful marine majesties he portrayed in several media, are unmatched to this day.

Winslow Homer was born in Boston in 1836 and moved to the then-pastoral suburb of Cambridge when he was six. He engaged in the boyhood pastimes of hunting and fishing that would become the subject and source of inspiration for his future paintings, but it was his close family relationships that would temper his talent to its full strength.

Winslow was the second son of Charles Savage and Henrietta Benson Homer. His father was a Boston dry goods merchant with an independent spirit. When Winslow was 13 his father set off for the West to join the Gold Rush. Although he did not find his fortune (and had to call his wife to retrieve him upon his return to Boston because he could not afford to pay for transport to Cambridge), he always looked the part of a successful businessman. Winslow would inherit his desire for autonomy as well as his dapper demeanor.

Henrietta Benson Homer enjoyed painting as a pastime and focused particularly on botanical illustrations. She completed a skillful series of floral studies in watercolor, several of which Winslow kept in his studio throughout his life. She encouraged her son in his artistic inclinations and was understandably proud of his accomplishments.

When he was 19, on his father's recommendation, Winslow went to Bufford's printmaking establishment in Boston, where he served as an apprentice lithographer for $5 a week and loathed every minute of it. He drew title pages to sheet music, including "Katy, Darling" and "Oh, Whistle and I'll Come to You, My Lad".

When his two-year apprenticeship was over Winslow learned woodblock engraving techniques from a French cutter named Damoreau, with whom he had made an acquaintance. Homer then rented a studio in Ballou's Publishing House Building in Boston and did freelance illustrations for *Ballou's Pictorial*. His engravings described topical street scenes and city amusements under such titles as *The Fountain on Boston Common*, *Emigrant Arrival at Constitution Wharf* and *Class Day at Harvard University in Cambridge*. One, entitled *Cambridge Cattle Market*, of July, 1859, suggests how rural this now-bustling city was when Homer lived and worked there.

Right: Winslow Homer in the year of his birth, 1836.

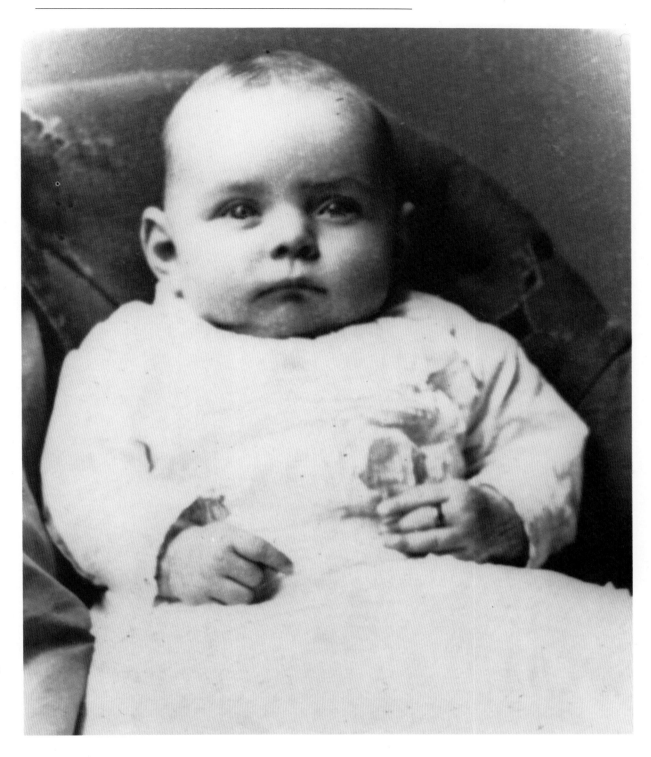

Opposite left: Henrietta Maria Benson Homer.

Opposite right: Charles S. Homer, Sr.

During this time Homer also contributed work to the popular publication *Harper's Weekly*. This professional association would continue for several years and provide income, exposure and travel opportunities for the young artist. However, when *Harper's Weekly* offered Winslow a salaried, staff position, he was not interested and remarked, "I declined it because I had had a taste of freedom. From the time that I took my nose off that lithographic stone, I have had no master; and never shall have any."

In the fall of 1859 Winslow moved to New York City, where he would find a bright studio apartment in the New York University Building on Washington Square. His engraving *(sic)* *Skating on the Ladie's Skating Pond in the Central Park, New York* reveals Homer's gift for gesture and interest in active movement. Our attention is drawn immediately into the swirl of skaters swinging their arms and legs left and right.

Harper's Weekly sent Homer to Washington to illustrate the inauguration of Abraham Lincoln in January of 1861, and his crowd-filled versions of the event show the splendor of the ceremonies in the vicinity of the White House and still-domeless Capitol. A few months later, after the Civil War had begun, Winslow would journey to the Army of the Potomac as a special artist correspondent.

Winslow's salary from *Harper's Weekly* was $30 a week plus railroad expenses. Although he did not witness any major battles, he finished a number of camp sketches. A letter from his mother to his younger brother, Arthur, on October 28, 1861, relates his experiences and her pride in his achievement. "We hear often from Win . . . he scaled a parapet while out sketching . . . and the only wonder is that he was not shot – his head popping up on such high places . . . he is very happy and collecting material for future greatness".

Another letter later in the same year indicates the way the family rallied around Winslow and supported his artistic ventures. Henrietta again writes to Arthur about his brother: "Perhaps you, even you, will be able to contribute towards a loan I

The bearer, Mr. Winslow Homer, is a special artist attached to Harpers Weekly, and is at present detailed for duty with the Army of the Potomac. Commanding Generals and other persons in authority will confer a favor by granting to Mr. Homer such facilities as the interests of the service will permit for the discharge of his duties as our artist-correspondent.

Harper & Brothers

hope to get up for him this winter to go abroad in the Spring, as he so desires to go for improvement, and he will be able to repay with principal and interest before many years, so write me about it."

Winslow made several trips back and forth from New York to Virginia to gather material for his Civil War engravings, and when in New York he attended night school at the National Academy of Design, where he enrolled in life classes. He also studied painting with Frederic Rondel, a Boston artist in New York, who taught him the rudiments of oil painting. Homer's first subjects were the various soldiers, sharpshooters and skirmishes he saw while at the front.

One of his first paintings, *The Sharpshooter*, was bought by his older brother, Charles, without Winslow's knowledge. Charles did this so that Winslow would not become discouraged and abandon his new direction for the safety, security and monotony of full-time illustration at *Harper's Weekly*.

Charles had presented Winslow with a copy of M.E. Chevreul's *The Laws of the Contrast of Color* when he had first moved to New York, and the artist referred to it frequently. He later commented about its theories to a friend: "It is my bible". The treatise described both how colors interact with one another and how they are perceived by viewers. Chevreul advocated vibrant, dynamic color selections, for he felt that viewers desire this piquancy in a way that "is essentially analogous to the inclination we have for food and drink of a flavor and odour more or less pungent."

Winslow used his sketches from the battlefront as the basis for oil paintings, some of which were small vignettes of the activities of camp life with titles such as *The Surgeon at Work, Punishment for Intoxication, Halt of a Wagon Train, The Game of Cards* and *The Bright Side.* The resplendent colors in some of these works – and notably in the Zouave uniforms in *The Brierwood Pipe* – clearly show the influence of Chevreul's ideas.

Throughout the duration of the conflict Homer would contribute engravings to *Harper's Weekly,* and each year he displayed several of his paintings at the National Academy of Design. Even after the war ended in April, 1865, Homer continued working on canvases inspired by his wartime experiences, and several of these would be among his most memorable.

On May 9, 1866, Homer received a diploma from the National Academy of Design certifying that he had attained the rank of Academician. At this time he exhibited his oil *Prisoners from the Front* in the Academy's Forty-first Annual Show. This painting, along with *On the Bright Side,* a relaxed rendering of four black soldiers resting by a camp tent, was selected to be sent to Paris for display in the American section of the Universal Exposition of 1867. Accordingly, Homer and a fellow Boston painter, Albert Kelsey, sailed for Europe aboard the ship *Africa* in December, 1866.

The Paris exposition brought a measure of international recognition to Winslow Homer. A reviewer for the *London Art Journal* wrote: "Certainly most capital for touch, character and vigour, are a couple of little pictures taken from the recent war, by Mr. Winslow Homer of New York. These works are real: the artist paints what he has seen and known."

While in Paris, Homer visited the Louvre galleries and attended various art students' *soirées* and casino balls, sketches of which he sent back to *Harper's Weekly* in New York. He also had the opportunity to study the styles of his French contemporaries, but about the degree of their influence on his work we can only theorize. His genre paintings certainly have a kin-

ship with the peasant subjects of Millet, and his version of a French farm bears a resemblance to the gentle landscape reveries of Corot. Later on, the flat compositional planes of Manet's canvases and portraits may have influenced Homer's placement of figures, and possibly Courbet's strong, realistic images of the French coastline, countryside and farmworkers find echoes in Homer's work. But all this is inferential at best, and in any case, Homer would soon become far too individual a painter to be understood in terms of influences or even comparisons.

Whatever affect his experiences in France may have had upon him, Winslow's independent, taciturn nature was ill suited to the fashionable gabble of salons and artists' coteries. He was far more inspired by the rugged terrain of his homeland and by the masculine pursuits of hunting and trapping, and he returned to America after only ten months.

Having recorded the devastation and sorrow of the Civil War, Homer now looked to places of rural charm and vacation pleasures to entertain his public. He continued to furnish black and white engravings for *Harper's Weekly* and expanded his illustrative repertoire to include several other magazines and publications, among them *Our Young Folks, Appleton's Journal* and *Every Saturday.* His subjects were young lads at play and pretty girls in frocks and ribbons, emblems of innocence and hope in America's future. Thus his oil painting *Snap the Whip* has the feckless gaiety of Mark Twain's *Tom Sawyer.* Although these barefoot boys have a sentimental appeal, the way Homer has organized their forms to focus our viewpoint reveals both his careful planning and a marked advance in his technique.

Mid-nineteenth century writers exulted in America's physical splendor and her distinctive mix of personalities and human types. The following words of Ralph Waldo Emerson in his essay "Self-Reliance" parallel Winslow Homer's emphasis on the indigenous qualities of his native land:

Opposite top: Homer sketched Mt. Vernon when he was on his way to join the Federal Army of the Potomac in Virginia in the summer of 1861.

Opposite bottom: Homer's Civil War press pass issued by *Harper's Weekly.*

Right: *The War for the Union, 1862 – A Cavalry Charge,* a wood engraving, based on a Homer sketch, that appeared in *Harper's Weekly.*

Left: A typical Homer Civil War sketch is his admirable *Cavalry Soldier on Horseback*, a study in black and white chalk on brown paper.

Above: *Homeward Bound*, one of Homer's post-war travel engravings for *Harper's*, is conventionally stilted but has a nice feel of the sea.

And why need we copy the Doric or the Gothic model? Beauty, convenience, grandeur of thought, and quaint expression are as near to us as any, and if the American artist will study with hope and love the precise thing to be done by him, considering the climate, the soil, the length of the day, the wants of the people, the habit and form of the government, he will create a house in which all these will find themselves fitted, and taste and sentiment will be satisfied also.

Newly-completed railroad lines made it possible for more people to travel to resort areas and wilderness territories that had previously been of limited access to tourists and those with a yearning for adventure. Some of these places, especially the Adirondacks, were popularized by the prints of Currier and Ives, and Homer's first North Woods scenes indicate a familiarity and common style with these reproductions. Homer visited country farms in upstate New York, and the watering places of the leisured classes in Long Branch, New Jersey, and Saratoga, New York. He also often journeyed to Gloucester, Massachusetts, to paint, a coastal site not far from the home of his brother, Charles, in West Belmont.

Just after the war the American Society of Painters in Watercolors was founded, and their annual exhibitions were a new opportunity for Homer. Watercolors were usually smaller and less expensive than oil paintings and were therefore more appealing and accessible to the buying public. An international exhibition in 1873 filled the entire National Academy of Design building in New York with almost 600 sketches from the United States and Europe. This display would bring critical attention and acclaim to the medium, and that in turn would benefit both the reputation and the finances of Winslow Homer, for the artist would shortly become one of watercolor's leading proponents and technical masters.

His early watercolors show a degree of care and finish that may have been related to the narrative detail required in Homer's professional illustrations. Explicit notations of sails, rigging and women's costumes were delicately drawn before washes of color were applied. At the same time, the bright, fresh colors and open air feeling of his rural and resort watercolor sketches are directly related to Homer's preference for on-the-scene painting. He discussed his methods with the art critic George Sheldon: "I prefer every time a picture composed and painted outdoors. This making studies and then taking them home to use them is only half right. You get composition but you lose freshness; you miss the subtle and, to the artist, the finer characteristics of the scene itself."

In February, 1879, Winslow sent 23 watercolors to the exhibition of the American Water Color Society, more than any other artist displayed, and he received this very favorable review from the *New York Times* critic on February 1, 1879: "His pictures have a vivid, fresh originality . . . childlike directness and naivete . . . He seems to be seldom or never bothered with the consideration of side issues, but hits straight at the mark and leaves the unimportant in a picture to take care of itself. Mr. Homer . . . must now take rank as one of the best of watercolorists."

In Homer's quest for new venues to explore pictorially, and perhaps tiring of the superficial nature of the pleasant, topical scenes he had created for the magazine illustrations, he set sail for England in the spring of 1881. The potential for this enterprise to expand the range and depth of the artist's talents, and the metaphor of the ocean's promise, is summed up in these lines by the nineteenth-century American poet, Henry Wadsworth Longfellow in his poem, "Possibilities":

Where are the stately argosies of song
   Whose rushing keels made music as they went
   Sailing in search of some new continent
   With all sails set, and steady winds and strong?
Perhaps there lives some dreamy boy, untaught
   In schools, some graduate of the field or street,
   Who shall become a master of the art. . . .

Winslow first went to London, where he sketched the Houses of Parliament. Then he traveled 275 miles north to the tiny fishing village of Cullercoats, near Tynemouth on the North Sea. Cullercoats was already established as an artist's colony, but its primary business was marketing the bounty of the sea hauled to shore by its fisherman.

Homer was fascinated with the women of the village, who became the heroines of the prolific series of drawings and watercolors he completed during his 20-month stay. (The men were rarely in sight, having gone to sea to procure their catch in the early hours of the day.) He was also intrigued by the vehemence of the ocean storms and rarely missed an opportunity to go out and explore when one of these tumultuous squalls resulted in a shipwreck. He painted several of these disasters, as well as recording the sufferings of the Cullercoats community in such sketches as *Perils of the Sea* and *The Dark Hour*.

Homer sailed home to New York in the fall of 1882, but the city environment could not hem him in for long. In the summer of 1883 he traveled to the southeastern shore of Maine, to a rocky, relatively barren peninsula known as Prout's Neck. Members of his family had been visiting this area of Maine for several years. His younger brother, Arthur, had honeymooned

Below left: *Winslow Homer, New York, 1880*, a portrait photograph by Napoleon Sarony.

Below: An artist's mannikin bought by Homer in Tynemouth during his English sojourn.

at Prout's Neck in 1875 and continued to return to the area every summer. In 1883 Charles Homer, Sr. bought up most of the land at Prout's Neck with financial support provided by his son, Charles, and soon a collection of houses and outbuildings became the family compound. Winslow would eventually remodel the stable into his permanent home and studio.

In the fall and winter of 1883 Winslow was back in New York, completing the final touches on an exciting oil painting entitled *The Life Line*. This work synthesized the dramatic storms the artist witnessed in England and made use of his figural studies of the Cullercoats women. In this large-scale canvas, a brawny rescuer bears the body of an unconscious young woman in his arms. The two central characters are borne by a breeches buoy, a fascinating rescue device for transporting people from ship to shore that Homer had first seen and sketched on a trip to Atlantic City, New Jersey. In the painting, however, we see only a portion of the buoy, and the ambiguity about how it is rigged and where, precisely, the shore is, heightens our sense of concern about the fate of the couple in the buoy's sling. Homer has captured a penultimate moment of dramatic action employing a minimum of compositional elements.

The *Life Line* was popular among the art critics in New York,

where the painting was first shown at the National Academy of Design, and it pleased the public as well. It was sold four days after it was first displayed in April, 1884, to a prominent collector, Catherine Lorillard Wolfe, heiress to the tobacco fortune, for $2500.

Winslow's mother, Henrietta Benson Homer, died in Brooklyn in that same April. In a move that would consolidate the family more closely after her loss, Homer gave up his New York apartment and settled in Maine the following summer. He would, however, make frequent trips to other places, including the Bahamas, Florida, Cuba and the Adirondack Mountains and Canada, and these settings would provide a variety of new and different perspectives, as well as plentiful fishing and hunting for the artist.

In December, 1884, Winslow sailed for the Bahamas with his father to gather drawings for an article about Nassau intended for *Century Magazine*. They stayed at the sumptuous Royal Victoria Hotel, and Winslow made numerous bright, lively watercolors that recorded the pleasures and beauties of the island and formed a kind of respite from the heroic battles against an unforgiving nature that dominated so many of his oil paintings. And in any case, pictures of gaiety and native pastimes were considerably more suitable for a travel and leisure publication.

Winslow journeyed from Nassau to Santiago de Cuba in February of 1885, and his sketches of this city are unusual in their concentration on architectural forms and flourishes. He was especially intrigued by the ancient forts and their cannons and ramparts, and he painted several pictures of Morro Castle, but, after five weeks the steamy tropical heat seems to have affected the New Englander. He wrote his brother, Charles: "No breakfast until 11, very bad smells, no drains, brick tiles and scorpions on the floor, and so hot that you must change your clothes every afternoon. I will be very glad to get home."

Winslow next began work on a series of ambitious marine paintings, which he would complete during the spring and fall seasons of 1885 and 1886 at Prout's Neck. He hired two local neighbors to pose as models for the men featured in *Eight Bells*, a scene of two sailors with sextants confirming their vessel's location at a quiet moment following a storm. One of the men was Henry Lee, first seen in *Life Line*, a handyman and carpenter who had first met Arthur Homer in Lowell, Massachusetts and had followed him to Prout's Neck. John Gatchell, the second sailor, was a native down-easter with a long beard, taciturn expression and seven sons. Winslow employed him for odd jobs and to pose for several paintings until Gatchell's penchant for

liquor made him too unreliable for this work.

Homer sent his watercolors of Nassau and Cuba to a dealer in New York, Reichard & Co., and included two of his recent oil paintings, *The Herring Net* and *Lost on the Grand Banks*. When the latter was exhibited at the National Academy of Design's annual exhibit in 1886 it was given this rave notice by the critic of *The Art Review*: "Winslow Homer shows in his *Lost on the Grand Banks* a rude vigor and grim force that is almost a tonic in the midst of the namby-pambyism of many of the other pictures. The utter simplicity of the composition, the fidelity to local coloring (and Mr. Homer's peculiar gamut of color never seemed more appropriate) and the spirited rendering of the wave-tossed boat and its anxious occupants – these are elements characteristic of Mr. Homer's work, but always welcome because Mr. Homer always has something to say."

Not only did Homer's relative isolation on the coast of Maine help to heighten his sense of the starkness of man's lonely, unrelenting struggle against the sea, he seemed genuinely to relish this privacy and anonymity and the absence of interruptions it provided. When summer resort visitors abandoned Prout's Neck in the fall he was always delighted. He wrote to his brother, Charles, "I like my home more than ever as people thin out".

Opposite: Winslow with his imperious father, Charles, and his dog, Sam.

Right: Homer indulging in his favorite recreation on the coast of Maine at Tautog.

On the other hand, the bitter winters of Maine were not always easy to endure, and Winslow made seven trips to Florida between 1885 and 1909. There he exchanged his panoramic visions for the particular, focusing in on the exotic species of flora and fauna he discovered on jaunts through the jungle.

Another American region that appealed to the outdoorsman and angler in Homer were the Adirondack Mountains of upstate New York. Winslow and his older brother, Charles, were founding members of the North Woods Club, a small fishing and hunting establishment not far from Minerva, New York, and the artist visited the area at least once a year during

most of the 1890s, his stays ranging from weeks to months. His avidity for fishing brought him out to the lakes at dawn, when the effects of sunrise over the tops of the mountains created rich color effects and moments of solitude and serenity that are beautifully captured in his pictures.

Photographs by Charles Homer of the artist in a canoe, and by Winslow of local Adirondack fishermen, indicate his ownership of a camera, and several of his watercolor sketches parallel the arrangement of forms in these black and white pictures. But photography cannot have contributed much to Homer's art. In addition to being monochrome and too static to capture the

movement he loved, it could never convey that sense of personal participation that makes so many of his canvases truly exciting.

Another northern hunting site that attracted Winslow and his brother, was the Tourilli Fish and Game Club on the Saguenay River, 100 miles north of Quebec City. The brothers were among a select group of 70 members, mostly Canadian, dedicated to the outdoors and tolerant of primitive living conditions in the wilds. The Homers visited Canada on several occasions during the summers between 1893 and 1902 and built a simple log cabin on the Tourilli Club's property. Winslow re-

lished the spartan living conditions and the new opportunities for both fishing and painting. As he wrote Charles after a winter visit, "The place suits me as if it was made for me by a kind of providence."

Homer's patrons in the 1890s were largely the successful businessmen, bankers and lawyers who sought the diversity of recreation and uncomplicated freedom of the Adirondacks during their days of leisure. The woods were unspoiled, the game was plentiful and the company was plain-spoken and knowledgeable. Among his significant collectors were Thomas B. Clarke, a retired banker and wealthy New York dealer, Joseph Choate and Samuel Untermeyer, both prominent New York lawyers, and Edward Hooper of Boston, a trustee of the Boston Museum of Fine Arts and the treasurer of Harvard College.

Each spring and fall during the 1890s, and 1900s Homer returned to Prout's Neck, working with renewed vigor on his major oil canvases. He painted images of this rugged shoreline during violent tempests in works such as *Northeaster* and *The Gale*, and he also dwelt on its native beauty in times of serenity, as in such canvases as *The West Wind* and *Moonlight, Wood's Island Light*. He showed a hunter with his game enjoying a moment of solitude in *Winter Coast*, as well as a brilliant red fox being chased by a throng of menacing crows in his haunting *The Fox Hunt*. In every case Homer selected subjects and sites he knew intimately and allowed his experience and the bravura of his brushstrokes to bring the scenes to life.

Once he rowed out on the bay beyond the Prout's Neck point and looked back at his home, capturing its unusual arrangement of shapes in a mystical reverie entitled *Artist's Studio in an Afternoon Fog*. Another of his later paintings, *Kissing the Moon*, reiterates an earlier theme of sailors swept up in the massive ocean swells off the coast, but this time he added a new twist by including the round white orb of the full moon, just touching the tip of a whitecap. His organizational facility and originality never failed him, any more than did his abiding love for his homeland.

Below: Homer, with palette and brushes in hand, talks with a neighbor outside the Prout's Neck studio.

Left: With Homer in this undated photograph is his favorite fishing companion, his brother Charles (r).

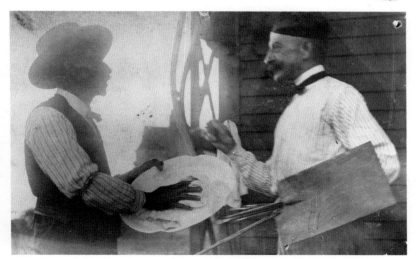

Saturday July 5th 1902
—Sent—

Shall send to Knoedler

Ten Water Colors —

cro 1 — "Colonies" if that is it — ·✗

2 — Street in Santiago ✗

3 — Spanish Club Santiago ✗

4 — Street corner. do —

○ 5 — turtle pound

6 — Turtle cay

7 — Bermuda Architecture

8 — Girls Pine point — ✗

9 — Bermuda Pigs

10 — after Tornado Texas —

(Knoedler comes in

To net me $200. each & all good or bad large or small

Winslow Homer was geographically isolated in Prout's Neck in his last two decades and, for the most part, alone in his artistic endeavors. Yet, he did enjoy the company of his family and the local tradesmen and townspeople who were year-round residents. All made their contributions to his life and work.

Zenas Seavey was a farmer who lived nearby, and Winslow would sometimes join the Seavey clan for dinner and, on occasion, ask them to visit his studio to see paintings in progress. Seavey was also the barber and trimmed Winslow's hair to his exacting standards. (He was almost entirely bald but would allow no one else to perform this duty.)

Leonard Libby was Homer's valet and the groundskeeper and all-around handyman at the family's Prout's Neck estate. His friendship with Winslow was borne of mutual respect and a loyal association over many years.

The stationmaster at Scarboro, Maine, Charles Walker, was a close friend and the man responsible for securing Homer's art supplies from Boston and New York, as well as the comestibles and the generous quantities of liquor furnished by establishments such as Boston's S.S. Pierce. Walker also had a penchant for photography, and he supplied several pictures of local venues for Winslow.

Homer spent a considerable amount of time with his father, who lived – and ruled the roost – until his death at the venerable age of 89. Charles Savage Homer, Sr. went on several trips to the tropics with Winslow and stayed at the main house at

Prout's Neck, called the Ark, for much of the year. Winslow dutifully attended to his father's imperious demands and indulged his idiosyncrasies, accepting his ways with a filial affection and concern. After spending the winter holidays with the octogenerian patriarch in Boston, Winslow wrote his sister-in-law, Mattie, in 1895: "Father and I have had a very pleasant Christmas – I shall go home tomorrow. I find that living with Father for three days, I grow to be so much like him that I am frightened. We get as much alike as two peas. . . ."

Winslow certainly shared his father's taste for fine haberdashery, as well as his passion for fishing and hunting, but, in addition to being brilliantly talented, the son was far more disciplined in his career and work habits than his father. It is hard to imagine the senior Homer devoting all those years to solitary industry at the easel.

There are no records or even very strong hints of any serious romantic relationship in Winslow's life, but he was clearly fond of women, and his work certainly contains many graceful renderings of female figures. He was especially drawn to the wife of his brother, Charles, a charming woman whom everyone called "Mattie". She was a faithful confidant and admirer of the artist, providing gentle encouragement, thoughtful gifts and sympathetic companionship, a softer, quieter influence in that masculine household. It is clear from his letters and the reminiscence of neighbors how deeply Winslow cherished their friendship.

Homer's true mistress was his work. Its production required an independent, detached style of existence that permitted travel to rough and sometimes dangerous parts of the world and long periods of secluded, introspective research. Homer labored consistently at his craft into his final decade. He enjoyed a robust constitution until his early 70s, and although his output slowed, he did not stop painting until his last year.

There is something rather haunting and sad about his last paintings. Homer simplified the compositional elements of later canvases such as *Cape Trinity, Saguenay River* and *Driftwood*. The former is an impressive landscape with an unusually emotive effect. A mountainous promontory projects into the night sea, with just a stroke of moonlight touching the clouds in the distance. The device of darkness highlights the awesome size of the cape but seems also to allude to a sense of twilight in the artist's life. *Driftwood* features the coast of Maine once more, but the small figure of a man by the shore, reaching out for the jetsam discarded by the waves, conveys a sense of isolation. The viewer feels somehow stranded and yet, as always, aware of the magnitude of the ocean expanse.

In his later years, Winslow had been bothered by stomach illnesses and the frustration of his increasing frailty. He suffered a stroke in 1908 but recovered enough to finish *Driftwood* in 1909. Afterward, he hung up his brushes and palette on the wall. He died in his studio on September 29th, 1910, not far from the restless sea, source of his greatest joy in life and of the magnificent legacy that would carry his name and his vision through the centuries.

Opposite: In this page from his daybook Homer records sending ten (now priceless) watercolors to M. Knoedler and Company, his dealer in New York City.

Below: This stolid portrait photo is probably the best-known image of Homer, a good example of why an artist's work is his best memorial.

The Veteran in a New Field
1865, oil on canvas, 24⅛×38⅛ in.
Bequest of Miss Adelaide Milton de Groot,
The Metropolitan Museum of Art, New
York, NY
(67.187.131)

CIVIL WAR AND GENRE

Winslow Homer's primary involvement in the Civil War was as an artist correspondent for the magazine *Harper's Weekly*. Although he was not much exposed to battle, he shared with the soldiers the rigors of the harsh physical and hygienic conditions found among the encampments near the front.

The material he gathered for the black and white magazine illustrations and the valuable insights he gained participating in the trials of the war would be evident in his more ambitious oil paintings. One of the best of these, *The Brierwood Pipe* makes superb use of M. Chevreul's principles set forth in *The Laws of the Contrast of Color*. Two soldiers of the Zouave regiment are shown whittling and smoking pipes, their brilliant red pantaloons highlighted against their deep blue jackets. This color resonance, as well as such details as their festive tasselled caps and fancy leggings, are the focus of the scene. These elements add visual interest and a certain gaiety to the dreariness of camp life.

In April, 1865, Confederate General Robert E. Lee surrendered his forces in Virginia and General Joseph Johnston surrendered to Union General William Tecumseh Sherman in North Carolina. Homer's painting *Veteran in a New Field* reflects the end of the conflict. It is a simple, poetic statement. A former soldier has tossed his jacket and canteen aside, and we see him from the back, cutting wheat with a scythe. His acres of untilled land and the horizon stretch wide before him, signaling the peace and possibilities of the future.

One of Homer's most famous and highly lauded paintings of the Civil War was *Prisoners from the Front* of 1866, a portrait of the Union leader Major General Francis Barlow receiving three Confederate soldiers in surrender. It is a scene without exciting action or schematic devices, yet a kind of nobility and emotional drama pervades the canvas. Homer expertly characterizes the range of personalities involved in the war, from the young, uncertain boy being captured to the bearded old man, humbly submitting to his fate, to the proud challenging stance of the third man still dressed in Confederate uniform. We feel the tension between Barlow and the Confederated soldier, yet it never threatens the stability of the image. Homer seemed to emphasize the sense of unity and spirit of a nation acknowledging a new direction.

Prisoners from the Front was sold directly out of the annual show at the National Academy of Design to John Taylor Johnston, who later was named the first president of the Metropolitan Museum of Art. The painting was then sent for display to the World Exposition in Paris, France, in the winter of 1866-1867. Homer followed its journey to Europe and stayed on the continent sightseeing and exploring for ten months.

After his return from France, Homer set his sights and talents on lighthearted scenes and vacation locales to produce his magazine illustrations and to provide subject matter for his paintings. Leisure activities such as croquet at the shore in Long Branch, New Jersey, hiking and horseback riding near Mt. Washington, New Hampshire, watching the races at Saratoga, New York, and trapping in the Adirondacks are among the resort compositions he presented to his audience.

During the 1870s Homer made many watercolor sketches of Houghton Farm in Mountainville, New York, a property belonging to Lawson Valentine, a patron from Brooklyn, New York. Here Homer captured the light playing over meadows with quick dots of the brush. His sensitivity to the sweetness and timeless pace of childhood can be seen in the gestures and expressions of his figures.

Homer also visited his brother, Charles, in West Townsend, Massachusetts, and painted many views of Gloucester, a small town on the ocean north of Boston. Ladies with parasols, boys sailing cat-boats and varied seaside diversions are his topics of his drawings and watercolors. Such titles as *Clam Bake, High Tide* and *The Bathers* convey the carefree spirit of these works.

In the summer of 1880 Homer's predilection for privacy and his growing interest in marine studies led to his move to a lighthouse on Ten Pound Island in the bay off Gloucester. Now his watercolors became freer and more impressionistic; mood had become as important as technical accuracy. In his words, "You must not paint everything you see. You must wait, and wait patiently, until the exceptional, the wonderful effect or aspect comes. . . ."

The Briarwood Pipe
1964, oil on canvas, 16⅞×14¾ in.
Mr. and Mrs. William H. Marlatt Fund,
The Cleveland Museum of Art, OH
(44.524)

The Brush Harrow
1865, oil on canvas, 23×37½ in.
Anonymous gift,
The Fogg Art Museum, Harvard University,
Cambridge, MA
(1939.229)

Prisoners from the Front
1866, oil on canvas, 24×38 in.
Gift of Mrs. Frank B. Porter,
The Metropolitan Museum of Art, New
York, NY
(22.207)

The Croquet Game
1866, oil on canvas, 6¼×10¼ in.
Friends of American Art Collection,
© *1988 The Art Institute of Chicago, IL*
(1942.35)

The Croquet Match
1867-69, oil on panel, 9¾×15¾ in.
Daniel J. Terra Collection,
Terra Museum of American Art, Chicago,
IL
(32.1985)

Long Branch, New Jersey
1869, oil on canvas, 16×21¾ in.
Charles Henry Hayden Fund,
Museum of Fine Arts, Boston, MA

Eaglehead, Manchester, Massachusetts
(High Tide: The Bathers)
1870, oil on canvas, 26×38 in.
Gift of Mrs. William F. Milton, 1923,
The Metropolitan Museum of Art, New
York, NY
(23.77.2)

A Rainy Day in Camp
1871, oil on canvas, 19⅞×36 in.
Gift of Mrs. William F. Milton,
The Metropolitan Museum of Art, New
York, NY
(23.77.1)

Shipbuilding at Gloucester
1871, oil on canvas, 13½×19¾ in.
Purchased 1950
Smith College Museum of Art,
Northampton, MA

Pages 34-35:
Snap the Whip
1872, oil, 22×36 in.
Purchase, 1919,
The Butler Institute of American Art,
Youngstown, OH

Sunlight and Shadow
1872, oil on canvas, 15¾×22½ in.
Gift of Charles Savage Homer,
Cooper-Hewitt Museum, The Smithsonian
Institution's National Museum of Design,
New York, NY
(1917-14-7)

Gloucester Harbor,
1873, oil on canvas, 15⁹⁄₁₆×22⁷⁄₁₆ in.
Gift of the Enid and Crosby Kemper
Foundation,
The Nelson-Atkins Museum of Art, Kansas
City, MO
(F76-46)

Three Boys on the Shore
1873, gouache and watercolor on paper,
7½×13¼ in.
© *Daniel J. Terra Collection,*
Terra Museum of American Art, Chicago,
IL
(6.1982)

The Dinner Horn
1875, oil on canvas, 11⅞×14¼ in.
Gift of Dexter M. Ferry, Jr.,
© *The Detroit Institute of Arts, MI*
(47.81)

Boys in a Pasture
1874, oil on canvas, 15¼×22½ in.
Charles Henry Hayden Fund,
Museum of Fine Arts, Boston, MA
(53.2552)

Left:
Taking Sunflower to Teacher
1875, watercolor on paper, 7×5⅞ in.
Eva Underhill Holbrook Collection of
American Art, Gift of Alfred H. Holbrook,
Georgia Museum of Art, University of
Georgia, Athens, GA
(945.50)

The New Novel
1877, watercolor, 9½×20½ in.
Museum of Fine Arts, Springfield, MA

Breezing Up (A Fair Wind)
1876, oil on canvas, 24⅛×38⅛ in.
Gift of the W. L. and May T. Mellon
Foundation,
National Gallery of Art, Washington, DC
(1943.13.1)

Left:
Fresh Air
1878, watercolor over charcoal,
20 1/16 × 14 1/16 in.
Dick S. Ramsay Fund,
The Brooklyn Museum, NY
(41.1087)

Pumpkin Patch
1878, watercolor, 14 × 20 in.
Canajoharie Library and Art Gallery, NY

Eastern Point Light
1880, watercolor over pencil, 9⅝×13⅜ in.
Gift of Alastair B. Martin,
The Art Museum, Princeton University, NJ
(57-116)

Sailboat and Fourth of July Fireworks
1880, watercolour and white gouache on
white paper, 9⅝×13⅝ in.
Bequest of Grenville L. Winthrop,
The Fogg Art Museum, Harvard University,
Cambridge, MA
(1943.305)

Hark! The Lark
1882, oil on canvas, 36⅜×31⅜ in.
Layton Art Collection, Gift of Frederick Layton,
Milwaukee Art Museum, WI
(L99)

Pages 54-55:
Watching the Tempest
1881, watercolor, 13⅞×18¾ in.
Bequest of Grenville L. Winthrop,
The Fogg Art Museum, Harvard University,
Cambridge, MA
(1943.296)

CULLERCOATS AND EARLY SEA PAINTINGS

By the 1880s Homer had achieved both a significant measure of recognition and a fairly steady income from his illustrations and watercolors. He seems, however, to have grown impatient with the casual subject matter of many of these drawings and sketches, with their emphasis on transitory moments of amusement. His months alone at the lighthouse on the bay off Gloucester may have awakened a desire for more challenging themes and deepened his interest in the mysteries of the sea.

In March, 1881, Winslow sailed to England and, after a brief visit to London, settled in Cullercoats, a little fishing village outside Tynemouth on the North Sea. He exchanged his silk hat and dress suits for the simple garb of the fishermen and went about the town with his sketching block to draw and paint the members of this tightly knit working community. Some of his efforts depict rugged female figures engaged in the labor of mending nets, carrying heavy loads of fish in wicker creels or waiting anxiously for the return of their menfolk from the ocean.

This rocky area of the coast was also the site of many shipwrecks, a cause for anguish among the townspeople but a dramatic occasion for an artist. Homer's presence during one of these perilous events is recorded in the watercolor *Watching the Tempest*. A fellow artist in residence at Cullercoats, George Horton, recounted Homer's appearance on the beach during a storm in October, 1881, when the vessel *Iron Crown* went aground: "As I stood watching the rescue operations, a little cab turned up with an old Cullercoats fisherman on the dicky: out stepped a dapper, medium-sized man with a watercolor sketching block and sat down on the ways. He made a powerful drawing with charcoal and some pastel. It was a brilliant drawing, the sea gray-green and the rest brown tone and in the middle distance, he set the lifeboat."

The women Homer painted were strong, full-bodied characters. He hired a local girl, red-haired Maggie Jefferson, for a shilling a sitting to pose as a model for his paintings. His lasses wore thick, flannel dresses, usually navy blue, and sturdy heavy-soled shoes that could weather the seasons and elements at Cullercoats. These fishergirls looked larger-than-life, with the three dimensional gravity, the stance and the pale skin tones of sculptured Grecian goddesses.

Homer's boats were thick-planked, flat-bottomed dories with square brown sails, their simple, generously curved proportions a suitable accompaniment for the sturdy people who manned them, and their plain, broad outlines ideal for deep-hued watercolor washes. The masses of dark clouds in the skies over Cullercoats and the infinite stretches of foam-marbled waves combined to give Homer backgrounds of exceptional power for virtually any composition he chose.

Winslow spent the fall and winter of 1883 at his studio in New York finishing a magnificent oil, *The Life Line*, a kind of summation of his studies of the ocean and its dynamic forces in Tynemouth. On a visit to Atlantic City, New Jersey, in 1883 Homer had made a series of sketches of a rope, canvas and pulley contraption known as a breeches buoy, and this rescue apparatus, bearing a man with his arms wrapped around a seemingly unconscious young woman, forms the central focus of the painting. Where the two ends of this lifeline are made fast is only suggested; apparently it runs from shore to a foundering ship, but the painting concentrates exclusively on the man and woman, whose red shawl whips across the face of her rescuer, matching the fury of the sea. By simplifying the elements selected for inclusion in the canvas, Homer hugely magnifies their presence.

After a journey to Nassau and Cuba to furnish illustrations for a travel article, Winslow returned to Prout's Neck and embarked on several masterly oil paintings during 1885 and 1886. His continuing fascination with the ocean found expression in such famous works as *Herring Net, Fog Warning, Lost on the Grand Banks* and *Eight Bells*. When the artist delivered 42 watercolors of Nassau and Cuba to his dealer, Reichard and Co., in New York, he also included two of these paintings and received lavish critical reviews.

In these marine epics we see the simple forms of fishermen in bulky oilskin coats and bell-shaped rainhats. Sweeping waves seem to rock across the picture plane, meeting the rugged wood boats at midpoint. Homer juxtaposes large masses and shapes in these paintings to create tension and visual interest, and his colors are somber and menacing, light colors being used only to clarify contours or highlight a detail. The results are nearly as majestic as the sea itself.

Afterglow
1883, watercolor on paper, 14¼×21 in.
Bequest of William P. Blake in memory of his
mother, Mary M. J. Dehon Blake,
Museum of Fine Arts, Boston, MA
(47.1202)

Returning Fishing Boats
1883, Watercolor and white gouache over
graphite, 15⅞×24¾ in.
Anonymous gift,
The Fogg Art Museum, Harvard University,
Cambridge, MA
(1939.233)

The Herring Net
1885, oil on canvas 29¼×47⅜ in.
Mr. and Mrs. Martin A. Ryerson Collection,
© *1989 The Art Institute of Chicago, IL.*
All rights reserved.
(1937.1039)

The Life Line
1884, oil on canvas, 28¾×44⅝ in.
The George W. Elkins Collection,
Philadelphia Museum of Art, PA
(E'24-4-15)

A Wall, Nassau
1898, watercolor and pencil on paper,
14¾×21½ in.
Amelia B. Lazarus Fund, 1910,
The Metropolitan Museum of Art, New
York, NY
(10.228.9)

THE TROPICS

In the winter of 1884 *Century Magazine* hired Winslow Homer as a freelance illustrator to furnish sketches of Nassau in the Bahamas, since tropical locales were increasing desirable resort destinations for wealthy American travelers. Homer and his father spent several months in Nassau, and the artist made a side trip to Cuba as well.

His watercolors highlight the clean, spare architectural lines of the native huts, the bountiful shapes of palm trees, native women in kerchiefs bearing fruit and the dazzling blue waters where sponge divers searched the depths. The half-naked torsos of these muscular black men at work became almost sculptural figures in Homer's sketches, and these studies would be practice exercises for future compositions of dramatic action. Several early sketches of sharks surrounding an abandoned boat, as well as a watercolor sketch of a native sailor stranded in similar circumstances, would form the structural basis for Homer's 1899 dramatic masterpiece *The Gulf Stream*.

Freshness and sensual delight in the simple, colorful island way of life is apparent throughout in Homer's renderings. There is an immediacy about these watercolors that cannot be found in the artist's oil paintings. A close-up view of ripe oranges on a branch makes the viewer feel like reaching out and picking them. At times it almost seems as if Homer had waded into the ocean to paint the native divers and fishermen – no distance or distraction interferes with our view of their endeavors.

Homer's Cuba sketches are somewhat different, focusing heavily on architectural forms and ornamentation. In Santiago de Cuba, Homer painted watercolors of the fancy iron grill-work, rhythmic rows of arches and tile-roofed stucco buildings of Santiago's Spanish heritage. He also was much taken with Cuba's military sites and painted several views of Morro Castle. The maize- and gray-colored hues he used to render the stone of the local houses were more subdued than his brilliant Nassau palette, but they effectively conveyed the historic feeling of Cuba's ancient streets.

Later, in the 1880s, the cold Maine winters proved too much even for Homer's hearty constitution, and he took his father and their fishing paraphenalia to Florida on several occasions, visiting Tampa, the Everglades, Enterprise and, finally, Key West. His Florida sketches lure us into the exotic realms of jungle, Spanish moss and splendidly feathered egrets. A marvelous perspective of coconut palms in Key West makes the viewer feel as if he were perched in the topmost branches of these regal trees. On the other hand, *Rowing Home* of 1890 is almost abstract. This scene of sunset on a bay consists of a series of transparent, horizontal washes of soft peach, blue and pale orange, with just a brief notation of three figures in a boat. It exemplified a moment of light and nuance very like the shimmering seascapes of the Impressionists.

Homer also visited the British isle of Bermuda on two occasions, in the winters of 1899 and 1901. His pictorial interest was primarily in the unusual coral reefs, the exotic native vegetation and flowers and the simple sandstone houses, often washed with pastel hues or painted dazzling white. The Bermuda sketches are serene and buoyantly colorful, even playful, as in the rendering of wild pigs called *Bermuda Settlers*. Like the Florida pictures, here Homer's sense of reprieve from the rigors of the Maine winter is almost palpable.

At Tampa
1885, watercolor, 14×20 in.
Canajoharie Library and Art Gallery, NY

In a Florida Jungle
c. 1885-1886, watercolor over graphite on
off-white woven paper, 14×20 in.
Worcester Art Museum, MA
(1911.19)

Pages 66-67:
A Norther, Key West
1886, watercolor, 13¼×19⅝ in.
Achenbach Foundation for Graphic Arts,
Gift of Mr. and Mrs. John D. Rockefeller 3rd,
The Fine Arts Museums of San Francisco,
CA
(1979.7.54)

Left:
Palm Tree, Nassau
1898, watercolor on paper, 23⅜×15 in.
Amelia B. Lazarus Fund, 1910,
The Metropolitan Museum of Art, New
York, NY
(10.228.6)

The Turtle Pound
1898, watercolor over pencil, 14¹⁵⁄₁₆×21⅜ in.
Sustaining Membership Fund; A. T. White
Memorial Fund; A. Augustus Healy Fund,
The Brooklyn Museum, NY
(23.98)

Sloop, Nassau
1899, watercolor on paper, 15×21½ in.
Amelia B. Lazarus Fund, 1910,
The Metropolitan Museum of Art, New
York, NY
(10.228.3)

Pages 72-73:
Salt Kettle: Bermuda
1899, watercolor over graphite, 13¹⁵⁄₁₆×21 in.
Gift of Ruth K. Henschel in memory of her
husband, Charles R. Henschel,
National Gallery of Art, Washington, DC
(1975.92.15)

Flower Garden and Bungalow, Bermuda
1899, pencil and watercolor, 13⅝×20½ in.
Amelia B. Lazarus Fund, 1910,
The Metropolitan Museum of Art, New York,
NY
(10.228.10)

Bermuda Settlers
1901, watercolor over graphite on cream
woven paper, 13⅞×21 in.
Worcester Art Museum, MA
(1911.12)

The Gulf Stream
1899, oil on canvas, 28⅛×49⅛ in.
Wolfe Fund, 1906. Catherine Lorillard Wolfe
Collection,
The Metropolitan Museum of Art, New
York, NY
(06.1234)

Key West
1903, watercolor over graphite on white
woven paper, 13¾×21⅜ in.
Gift of Edward W. Forbes,
The Fogg Art Museum, Harvard University,
Cambridge, MA
(1956.210)

Key West: Hauling Anchor
1903, watercolor over graphite, 14×21⅞ in.
Gift of Ruth K. Henschel in memory of her
husband, Charles R. Henschel,
National Gallery of Art, Washington, DC
(1975.92.9)

Homosassa Jungle
1904, watercolor over graphite on white
paper, 13⅝×21⅜ in.
*Gift of Mrs. Charles S. Homer in memory of
the late Charles S. Homer and his brother,
Winslow Homer,
The Fogg Art Museum, Harvard University,
Cambridge, MA*
(1935.50)

Rowing Home
1890, watercolor on paper, 13¾×19⅞ in.
Acquired 1920,
The Phillips Collection, Washington, DC

The Guide
1889, watercolor on paper, 13⅝×19½ in.
Bequest of Charles Shipman Payson, 1988,
Portland Museum of Art, ME

Pages 84-85:
The Mink Pond
1891, watercolor over graphite on heavy
white woven paper, 14×21 in.
Bequest of Grenville L. Winthrop,
The Fogg Art Museum, Harvard University,
Cambridge, MA
(1943.304)

Adirondacks
and Canada

Winslow Homer was always an avid fisherman and hunter, and with his brother, Charles, he visited the Adirondack Mountains on several occasions. Together, they joined a club called the Adirondack Preserve Association for the Encouragement of Social Pastimes and the Preservation of Game and Forests, later happily shortened to the North Woods Club. When tourists began to swarm into Maine during the summer Winslow increasingly retreated to this attractive mountain wilderness near Minerva, New York.

Homer's Adirondack paintings convey the respect he felt for both the human and animal inhabitants of the territory. His woodsmen often appear alone, as straight and tall as the neighboring pines, or sometimes in pairs, sharing the bounty of the wilderness, fishing, hunting, canoeing or exploring. Similarly, Homer's facility in depicting animals in motion and at rest can be seen in his watercolors of hunting dogs on the trail, in boats, standing on logs or swimming. Stags and deer with delicate limbs and graceful bearing, even in the anguish of death, were another subject superbly described in the Adirondack series, as were the artist's renderings of leaping trout.

Homer's dedication to accuracy is reflected in his remarks about the oil painting *Hound and Hunter*, which shows a young man reaching out from a canoe for a stag's antlers while his dog swims rapidly in pursuit of the beast. He noted in a letter, "Did you notice the boy's hands – all sunburnt; I spent more than a week painting those hands." But the viewer – here, or in any of Homer's paintings – is never aware of the artist's deliberations and is only fleetingly aware of his technique. The scenes look

authentically spare, the colors are true and the beauty of the landscape strikes the viewer with an integrity undiluted by any distracting assertion of painterly craft.

Winslow and Charles also ventured farther north, into Canada, joining an elite group of fishermen and hunters at the Tourille Fish and Game Club located 100 miles north of Quebec City. The living conditions here were as spartan as those in the Adirondacks, and, once more, native inhabitants and activities provided the material for Homer's watercolors. He was particularly fond of portraying the local Montagnais Indians – building birchbark canoes, portaging their vessels across riverbanks and negotiating rapids in their search for "ouananiche," the prized local salmon. Homer often sought to define the singular identity of the region by focusing on one fisherman, one Indian, one bear, even one fish, to symbolize the independent soul of this distant northern region.

The authenticity of his style is evocatively described in the following review in the New York Times on April 9, 1898: "One feels the splendid swirl of the icy waters and the swift rush of the canoes down the foaming rapids – one almost hears the hurried staccato cries of the French guides as they steer the frail birchbark canoes through the seething billows, and anon, one hears the faint swish of the fisherman's line as he casts his fly at sunset on the mirrorlike black surface of the mountain lake.

Something of the vigor and vitality of the cold air of these northern latitudes has entered into the artist's brush." The challenge of matching Homer's painterly eloquence in prose was a daunting task, one this critic handled gracefully.

Sunrise, Fishing in the Adirondacks
1892, watercolor on wove paper,
13½×20½ in.
Achenbach Foundation for Graphic Arts
purchase,
Mildred Anna Williams Fund,
The Fine Arts Museums of San Francisco,
CA
(1966.2)

The Blue Boat
1892, watercolor on paper, 14¾×21¼ in.
Bequest of William Sturgis Bigelow,
Museum of Fine Arts, Boston, MA
(26.764)

Deer Drinking
1892, watercolor, 14¹⁄₁₆×20¹⁄₁₆ in.
The Robert W. Carle Fund,
Yale University Art Gallery, New Haven,
CT
(1976.36)

Hudson River – Logging
1892, watercolor and pencil, 14×20⅝ in.
*In the collection of the Corcoran Gallery of
Art, Museum Purchase,*
© *Corcoran Gallery of Art, DC*
(03.4)

Canoe in Rapids
1897, watercolor over graphite on white
paper, 13½×20½ in.
Louise E. Bettens Fund,
The Fogg Art Museum, Harvard University,
Cambridge, MA
(1924.30)

The Pioneer
1900, watercolor on paper, 13⅞×21 in.
Amelia B. Lazarus Fund, 1910,
The Metropolitan Museum of Art, New
York, NY
(10.228.2)

Montagnais Indians (Making Canoes)
1895, watercolor, 14×20 in.
Virginia Steele Scott Collection,
Huntington Library and Art Gallery, San
Marino, CA

Pages 96-97:
The Portage
1897, watercolor, 14×21 in.
Bequest of Dors M. Brixey,
Yale University Art Gallery, New Haven,
CT
(1984.32.17)

Winter Coast
1890, oil on canvas, 36×31⅝ in.
The John G. Johnson Collection,
Philadelphia,
Philadelphia Museum of Art, PA
(J#1004)

Pages 100-101:
West Wind
1891, oil on canvas, 30×44 in.
Addison Gallery of American Art, Phillips
Academy, Andover, MA

PROUT'S NECK
AND THE EPIC PAINTINGS

During the 1890s and early 1900s Homer's oils of Prout's Neck and its environs were increasingly concerned with the atmospheric effects of fog and storm. Human figures are often absent from these paintings, and their compositional structure and variegated streaks of light and dark hues sometimes approach abstraction. Masses of rocks, brilliant skies and swirls of sea foam are the departure points for Homer's amazing brushwork.

He mined the special quality of mist for its optical influence on landscape in *The Artist's Studio in an Afternoon Fog*. Here, the angular geometric shapes of his home echo the rugged Maine coastline. The violence of storms absorbed him in *Northeaster* and *The Gale*. Homer's special genius lay in defining the dynamic opposition of natural forces and in making the viewer almost palpably aware of the objective beauty and sublime power of this unleashed energy.

He rarely missed a chance to go out into a gale, and if he had visitors, they, too, were enlisted to join him. When John W. Beatty, director of the Carnegie Art Institute, was with Homer at Prout's Neck, Winslow dragged him along to witness the glory of nature's fury. "'Come,' he said, 'quickly! It is perfectly grand!'"

Homer was a stickler for precise handling of moments in time. He wrote in a letter to his dealer at Knoedler and Company in New York about the painting *West Point, Prout's Neck* of 1900: "The picture is painted 15 minutes after sunset – not one minute before – as up to that minute, the clouds over the sun would have their edges lighted with a brilliant glow of color, but now (in this picture) the sun has got beyond their immediate range and they are in shadow . . . You can see it took many days of careful observation to get this (with a high sea, and tide) just right."

Although Homer himself had retreated into relative seclusion at Prout's Neck during the 1890s, his epic oil paintings began to receive extensive recognition and acclaim from prominent art patrons and the general public. *The Gale* was awarded a gold medal at the World's Columbian Exposition in Chicago in 1893. In 1894 the Pennsylvania Academy of Fine Arts bought the grimly beautiful *The Fox Hunt* for its permanent collection of American art. In 1896 the Carnegie Institute in Pittsburgh awarded Homer a gold medal and cash purchase prize of $5000 for his oil painting *The Wreck*. This was both a significant honor and the highest price paid to date for one of his works. Winslow was then 60 years old, and his letter acknowledging congratulations from his foremost patron, Thomas Clarke, reveals a still vital interest in his profession: "Let us hope that it is not too late in my case to be of value to American art in something that I may yet do from this encouragement."

Thomas Clarke made a sizeable contribution to the monetary value and public awareness of Homer's paintings when he arranged an exclusive display of 25 of the artist's works at New York's Union League Club in March, 1898. The show paired Homer with another important American painter, George Inness, and elicited this comment from the *New York Tribune*'s reviewer: "Winslow Homer stands alone, and is, on the whole, as rare a figure as Millet or Delacroix, or Fortuny or Whistler. He broke new ground, painted familiar subjects as no one had ever painted them before him so that he seems to move in a world of his own." In his recollections of the artist in 1910 J. Eastman Chase, a well-respected dealer, confirmed the profoundly autonomous nature of Homer's work: "Homer was less influenced by others and by what others had done than any artist – any man, I may as well say – I have ever known."

The Metropolitan Museum of Art purchased Homer's tropical epic *The Gulf Stream* in 1906 from the annual display at the National Academy of Design in New York, and this strikingly forceful canvas soon became one of the artist's most famous and widely recognized oil paintings. Then the Carnegie Institute in Pittsburgh capped a decade of awards and distinction by staging a one-man retrospective exhibit of 22 paintings by Winslow Homer in 1908. The works spanned 30 years of the artist's career, and half of them were on loan from public institutions. Homer would have only two more years to live, but he already had the satisfaction of knowing that he had become one of the acknowledged masters of American art.

Fox Hunt
1893, oil on canvas, 38×68½ in.
Joseph E. Temple Fund,
The Pennsylvania Academy of the Fine Arts,
Philadelphia, PA
(1894.4)

The Gale
1893, oil on canvas, 30¼×48⅜ in.
Worcester Art Museum, MA
(1916.48)

Pages 104-105:
The Artist's Studio in an Afternoon Fog
1894, oil on canvas, 24×30¼ in.
R. T. Miller Fund,
Memorial Art Gallery of the University of
Rochester, NY
(41.32)

Moonlight, Wood Island Light
1894, oil on canvas, 30¾×40¼ in.
Gift of George A. Hearn in memory of
Arthur Hoppock Hearn, 1911,
The Metropolitan Museum of Art, New
York, NY
(11.116.2)

The Wreck
1896, oil on canvas, 30⅜×48⁵⁄₁₆ in.
The Carnegie Museum of Art, Pittsburgh,
PA
(96.1)

Early Morning After a Storm at Sea
1902, oil on canvas, 30¼×50 in.
Purchase from the J. H. Wade Fund,
The Cleveland Museum of Art, OH
(24.195)

Pages 110-111:
Northeaster
1895, oil on canvas, 34⅜×50¼ in.
Gift of George A. Hearn, 1910,
The Metropolitan Museum of Art, New
York, NY
(10.64.5)

LIST OF COLOR PLATES

Picture Credits

All pictures were provided by the credited museum or gallery, except for those supplied by the following:

Achenbach Foundation for the Graphic Arts, The Fine Arts Museums of San Francisco, CA: Winslow Homer, *The War for The Union, 1862 – A Cavalry Charge*, Wood engraving, *Harper's Weekly*, 6, no. 288, Gift of Dr. & Mrs. Robert A. Johnson: 9

Bowdoin College Museum of Art, Brunswick, ME, Gift of the Homer Family: 6(all three), 11(both), 12, 13, 14, 15, 16

Cooper-Hewitt Museum, The Smithsonian Institution's National Museum of Design, New York, NY: Winslow Homer, *Homeward-Bound*: 10(right)

Mount Vernon Ladies' Association, VA: 8(both)

Museum of Fine Arts, Boston, MA: Winslow Homer, *Cavalry Soldier on Horseback*, Black and white chalk on brown paper, Anonymous Gift: 10(left).

Acknowledgments

The publisher would like to thank the following people who helped in the preparation of this book: Don Longabucco, who designed it; Rita Longabucco, who did the picture research; and John Kirk, who edited the text.